Life on Mars

Mary Kay
Carson

SCHOLASTIC INC.

Library of Congress Cataloging-in-Publication Data
Carson, Mary Kay, author.
Life on Mars / by Mary Kay Carson.
Audience: Age 6–8. Audience: K to grade 3.
ISBN 9780545935487 (pbk.) ISBN 9781338029581 (ebook)
Mars (Planet)—Juvenile literature.
Inner planets—Juvenile literature.
QB641.C35277 2016   576.8—dc23   2016005382

ISBN 978-0-545-93548-7

10 9 8 7 6 5 4 3 2 1   16 17 18 19 20

Printed in the U.S.A. 40
First printing 2016

Contents

Welcome to Mars!

Astronauts have never been to Mars. But **robot spacecraft** have. We've learned a lot from them. Mars is a cold, **desert** world. Its rocks are orange-red because of rusty **iron minerals**.

It's a fact!

Mars looks reddish in the night sky. Look up and see for yourself!

That is why Mars is called the red **planet**.

NEW WORD

robot

ROH-bot

Robots are machines that do many important, sometimes dangerous jobs.

SAY IT OUT LOUD

Mars vs. Earth

Mars and Earth are neighbors. They are alike in some ways. Both planets have **ice caps**, seasons, and weather. They both have wind, clouds, and storms.

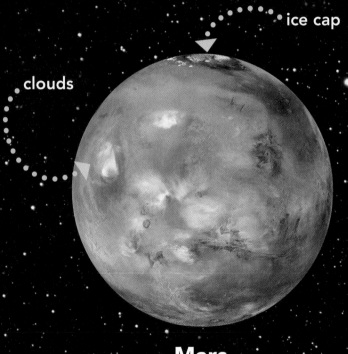

ice cap

clouds

Mars

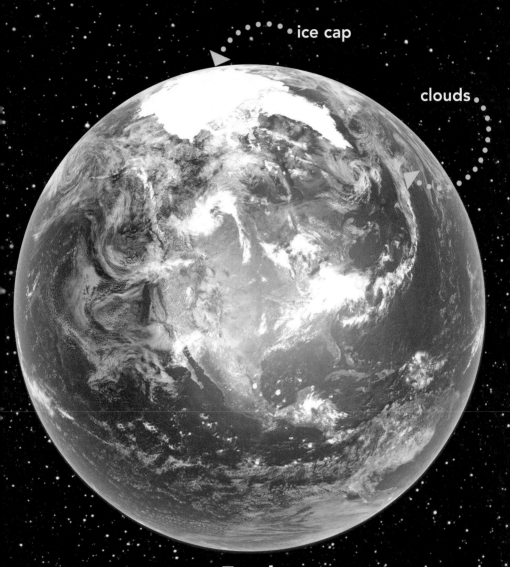

ice cap

clouds

Earth

But Mars and Earth have differences
as well.

Earth is almost twice the size
of Mars. Also, the two planets have
different **landscapes**. Earth is mostly
covered in oceans, and has rivers
and lakes, too. But Mars doesn't
have any of these. It is so cold that
all of the water has frozen to ice.

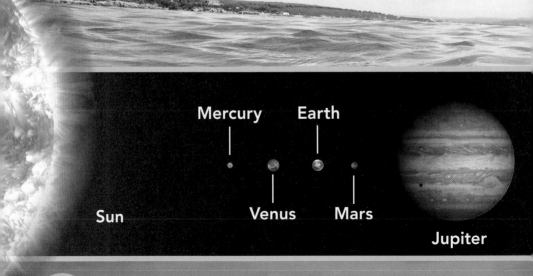

Sun

Mercury

Venus

Earth

Mars

Jupiter

Earth has **oxygen** in its **atmosphere**.
The plants and animals that live
on Earth need this oxygen to live.
However, Mars has very little oxygen.

So does anything live on Mars?
Scientists have been trying to find out.

Saturn   Uranus   Neptune

Movie Martians

Are there towns on Mars? A hundred years ago, many people thought so. **Telescopes** showed a world covered in land. Shouldn't people be living there? Some scientists agreed, until better telescopes and space missions proved them wrong.

It's a fact!

In 1896, **astronomer** Percival Lowell studied Mars through his telescope.

But people still like to imagine what life on Mars would be like. Over the years, there have been books about talking green Martians—and scary movies about them coming to Earth!

He thought he could see farms and **canals** on Mars. Many people believed him.

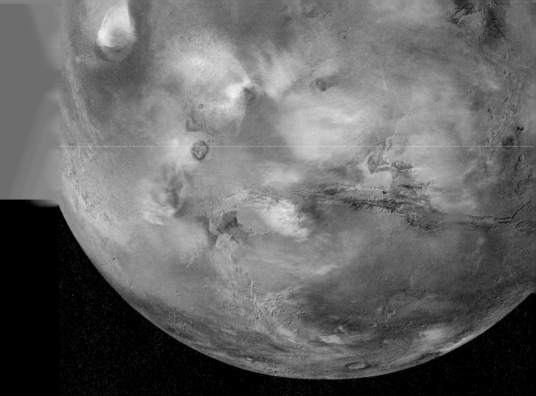

A Close-Up Look

Spacecraft began visiting Mars in the 1960s. Robot spacecraft measured the air and took pictures from space. No Martian towns were in the photos. There were no farms, forests, lakes, or animals. Mars seemed airless, waterless, and lifeless.

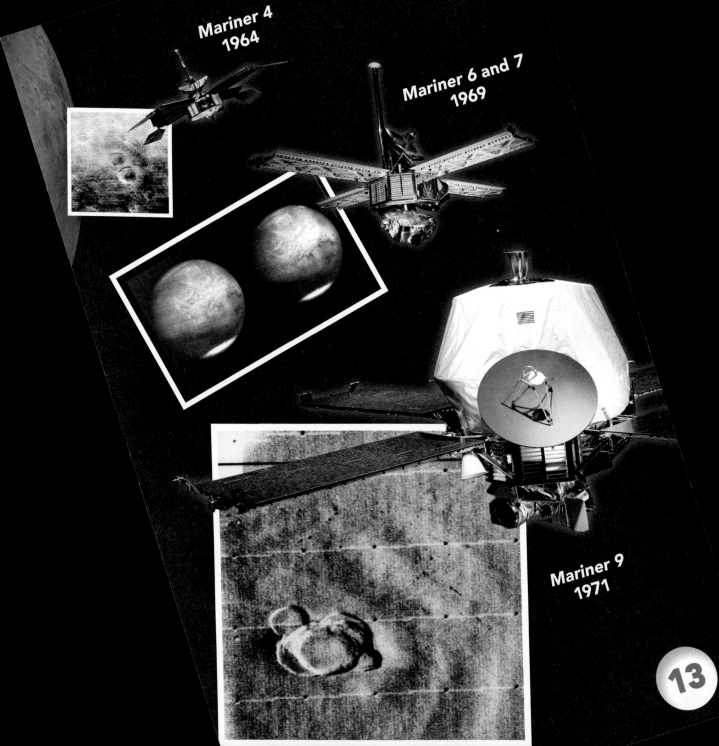

Mariner 4
1964

Mariner 6 and 7
1969

Mariner 9
1971

13

Not all life is easy to see. On Earth, worms live underground. Different types of **fungus** grow inside rocks. **Microbes** float in the air.

You can't see these forms of life from space. Perhaps life on Mars is tiny, or hidden. A spacecraft mission went to find out in 1976.

Viking 1 and *Viking 2* were the first spacecraft to land on Mars. Each robot scooped up soil and tested it. They did not find anything that was alive.

Follow the Water

Nothing living was in the *Vikings'* photos. The landscape was surprising, though. It looked like water *used* to flow there.

A spacecraft circling above Mars took this photo. Scientists believe it shows gullies, or ditches, created by running water.

There are bits of Mars on Earth!

The photos showed hillsides with steep ditches and dusty, dry riverbeds. Scientists wondered what it meant. Was Mars once warmer? Did it use to have lots of liquid water?

It's a fact!

Meteorites are space rocks that fell to Earth. Some of these rocks come from Mars.

How do you know what a place was like a billion years ago? On Earth, scientists study old rocks. On Mars, rovers are doing that job. Two rovers arrived on Mars in 2004. Their names were *Spirit* and *Opportunity*. Both had cameras, tools, and robot arms to study rocks.

It's a fact!

cameras

solar
panels

antennas

robot
arm

tools

Spirit and *Opportunity* landed on Mars
by bouncing down on giant airbags!

Spirit and *Opportunity* had a 90-day mission. **Engineers** thought that after three months the rovers' solar panels would be too dusty to work. But blowing winds cleaned the solar panels.

before

after

The rovers have now been on Mars for more than a **decade**! They have studied many rocks. Some rocks showed signs that they used to be underwater.

The rovers proved that Mars wasn't always a desert! Mars used to be warmer. Long ago, there was water. Rain fell. Seas and rivers flowed on Mars. Was there life back then, too?

What would Mars have looked like if it had water?

Plants and animals need water.
Even microbes need food.
And all life needs **nutrients**.

Could anything
grow on Mars?

In 2008, a spacecraft called *Phoenix* arrived on Mars. It landed near its north pole.

The spacecraft scooped up dirt. It tested it. It found nutrients, like **nitrogen**. It's too cold for life there now. But if Mars were warmer, microbes could live there!

north pole

Seeking Life Signs

Mars had the ingredients for life. But did these ingredients ever *make* life? Scientists are looking for clues. Some signs of past life would be **fossils** or substances called **organics**.

Organics are basic materials that make up all life. They are its building blocks. Organics can be found in everything from skin to stems and bark to **bacteria**.

A new rover, *Curiosity*,
arrived on Mars in 2012.
It is searching for organics
at the bottom of an ancient lake.
Curiosity is big—about
the size of a Jeep!

Today Mars is a tough place
for life as we know it. It is super
cold, very dry, and there isn't
much air. The amount of air in
the atmosphere is important.
Air is not just for breathing.

Earth's layer of air
protects life. It's like
a pair of sunglasses.
It keeps out dangerous
sun **rays**.

Mars doesn't have
this protection.
Powerful rays would
kill anything on the ground.

Dr. Nathalie Cabrol is a scientist who studies microbes that live in harsh places. She studies very cold places with little air and powerful rays from the sun. One example of this type of place is a lake high in the mountains. These places have similar **climates** to Mars. Everything Dr. Cabrol has learned about these microbes will help rovers look for them on Mars, too.

"There is no life possible at the surface of Mars today, but it might still be hiding underground."

ExoMars is a new mission to Mars. "Exo" is short for "exobiology," which is the study of alien life. An ExoMars rover will look underground for signs of life, below the reach of dangerous sun rays.

The rover will drill down more than six feet. Maybe life is safe there. The rover is scheduled to leave for Mars in 2018.

Is there life on Mars? Was there ever? There's no proof yet. Scientists are still searching.

Glossary

astronomer
A person who studies stars, planets, and space.

atmosphere
The mixture of gases that surrounds a planet.

bacteria
A tiny microbe that can be useful or harmful. (There are more bacteria than any other living thing on Earth.)

canal
A ditch made to carry water.

climate
The weather typical of a place over a long period of time.

decade
Ten years.

desert
A dry place where hardly any plants grow because there is so little rain.

engineer
Someone who is specially trained to design and build machines or large structures such as bridges and roads.

fossil
The bone, shell, or other trace of an animal or plant from millions of years ago preserved, or kept in its original state, as rock.

fungus
Plantlike living thing that doesn't have leaves, flowers, or roots, such as mushrooms and yeast.

ice cap
Thick layer of ice that covers an area of land, usually on the top and/or bottom of a planet.

iron
A hard metal found in many rocks.

landscape
A large area of land that can be seen in a single view.

meteorite
A rock from space that landed on Earth.

microbe
Living thing too small to be seen without a microscope.

mineral
A solid substance usually found in the ground that does not come from a living thing.

nitrogen
A gas plants need to grow.

nutrient
Food or other substance, like a protein or vitamin, that living things need to grow and live.

organic
Material that contains a chemical element called carbon. All living things are made of organics.

oxygen
A gas in the air that animals need to live.

planet
A large, round object that travels around a sun..

ray
Beam of light or energy.

robot
A machine that is programmed by humans to perform complex tasks.

spacecraft
A machine that travels into space.

telescope
A tool that makes faraway objects appear brighter, nearer, and larger.

Index

Images
Photographs ©: cover: JPL-Caltech/MSSS/NASA; back cover: forplayday/iStockphoto/Thinkstock; 1 center: forplayday/
iStockphoto/Thinkstock; 1 background: Igor Kovalchuk/Dreamstime; 2-3: Kim Briers/Shutterstock, Inc.; 4-5 top: NASA; 4
cartoon and throughout: Cory Thoman/Dreamstime; 5 bottom background: Paolo74s/iStockphoto; 5 bottom right: Galaxy
Picture Library/Alamy Images; 5 bottom left: Sean Locke Photography/Shutterstock, Inc.; 6 center: JPL-Caltech/MSSS/NASA;
6-7 background: Paolo74s/iStockphoto; 7 center: tombonatti/iStockphoto; 8 background: Gabriele Maltini/iStockphoto; 8
Sun: NASA; 8 Mercury: NASA; 8 Venus: NASA; 8 Mars: NASA; 8 Jupiter: NASA; 8 Earth: tombonatti/iStockphoto; 9
background: NASA; 9 Saturn: NASA; 9 Uranus: NASA; 9 Neptune: Elena Duvernay/Dreamstime; 10 top: Peter Kirschner/
Fotolia; 10 bottom center: J.E. Purdy, Boston/Library of Congress; 10 cartoon and throughout: Cory Thoman/iStockphoto; 11
top right: Pictorial Press Ltd./Alamy Images; 11 center right: Moviestore collection Ltd./Alamy Images; 11 top background:
Peter Kirschner/Fotolia; 11 bottom right: Scholastic Inc.; 12 top: JPL-Caltech/MSSS/NASA; 13 top left: NASA; 13 top right:
NASA; 13 center left: NASA; 13 center right: NASA; 13 bottom right: NASA; 14 top background:
kertlis/iStockphoto; 14 center grass: Okea/Dreamstime; 14 top inset: Pasieka/Science Source; 14 bottom: Auscape/Getty
Images; 15 bottom background: NASA; 15 bottom left: NASA; 15 bottom right: NASA; 15 top background: Paolo74s/
iStockphoto; 16-17 top: NASA; 16 bottom left: Nomadsoul1/Dreamstime; 16 bottom center: Manfred Kage/Science Source;
16 bottom right: MarcelC/iStockphoto/Thinkstock; 16 bottom background: Paolo74s/iStockphoto; 18-19 top: Dr. Timothy
Parker, JPL/NASA; 18 bottom right: Corby Waste/NASA; 19 center: NASA/Science Source; 20 center left: NASA; 20 center
right: NASA; 20 bottom right: NASA; 20-21 background: Jaysi/Dreamstime; 20 tape and throughout: spxChrome/
iStockphoto; 21 center left: Mark Garlick/Science Source; 21 center right: JPL-Caltech/MSSS/NASA; 22 top background: Juraj
Kovacik/Dreamstime; 22 center: Andy445/iStockphoto; 22 bottom right: NASA; 23 bottom: NASA; 23 center left: Science
Source; 23 center: NASA; 23 center right: NASA; 24 background: Penchan Pumila/Dreamstime; 24 skin: jaminwell/
iStockphoto; 24 hand: MBCheatham/iStockphoto; 24 bamboo: picamaniac/iStockphoto; 24 bark: HadelProductions/
iStockphoto; 24 bacteria: Eraxion/iStockphoto; 25 background: NASA; 25 center: NASA; 25 center right: MousePotato/
iStockphoto; 26 center: Aphelleon/Dreamstime; 26 bottom: Aphelleon/Shutterstock, Inc.; 27 bottom
left: High Lakes Project/SETI Institute/NASA; 27 center right: High Lakes Project/SETI Institute/
NASA; 27 background: NASA; 28 background planet: NASA; 28 center: NASA; 28-29 background
sky: Paolo74s/iStockphoto; 29 planet: NASA; 30 bottom left: NASA; 31 top right: NASA;
32 background: Dr. Timothy Parker, JPL/NASA.